ALABASTER

NLT.

ARTIST INTRODUCTION

Ruth is the story of a non-Israelite woman being brought into the fold—and how her offsprings were blessed. Likely written somewhere around the 5th century BCE, under Persian occupation, Ruth appears a counter to ancient stories in which marriages between Jewish men and non-Jewish women were broken up in the interest of "purity" (Ezra 9 and Nehemiah 13).

After the Babylonian captivity, in which the Israelites were exiled, many Israelites had intermarried with non-Jewish women. When the Jewish people were allowed to return to Jerusalem under the Persian empire, there was a crisis of identity—now that we have a homeland again, is it okay to be married and have children with non-Jewish people? Can someone who is not ethnically Jewish be considered one of us?

The story of Ruth is told within this historical context, bringing together an implausible pairing—a widowed Moabite woman and an older Jewish man. These two are brought to the center of Israelite history as the great-grandparents of the highly-regarded King David.

Many of these matters may correlate with our modern day. In an increasingly interconnected and global era, we are learning to live together across the world. To whom do each of us belong to and are held responsible for? To whom do we consider kin? To what extent do culture and traditions extend to those outside of its orthodoxy?

Ruth is a reminder that God moves and works in radically inclusive ways. While most characters draw their names from symbolic meanings within their own culture, Ruth's name stands alone with no clear symbolism—harkening to her status as a foreigner. And yet, despite this, she is welcomed as the center of the story.

In highlighting the themes of radical inclusion of Ruth, we choose a lilac violet color—often a symbol of compassion and spirituality—to motivate the design and image-making process. We carry this theme of inclusion into several visual motifs, placing images within each other and pairing unlikely materials, objects, and scenes together as an exploration of the unlikely, but beautiful blessed union found within Ruth.

As we read Ruth, may we reflect on our own stories, cultures, and traditions, and consider the invitation: to welcome those on the outside, to unequivocally behold them as our own family, to see everyone as kin. Amen.

BOOK OF

RUTH

1

ELIMELECH MOVES HIS FAMILY TO MOAB

¹ In the days when the judges ruled in Israel, a severe famine came upon the land. So a man from Bethlehem in Judah left his home and went to live in the country of Moab, taking his wife and two sons with him. ² The man's name was Elimelech, and his wife was Naomi. Their two sons were Mahlon and Kilion. They were Ephrathites from Bethlehem in the land of Judah. And when they reached Moab, they settled there.

[3] Then Elimelech died, and Naomi was left with her two sons. [4] The two sons married Moabite women. One married a woman named Orpah, and the other a woman named Ruth. But about ten years later, [5] both Mahlon and Kilion died. This left Naomi alone, without her two sons or her husband.

NAOMI AND RUTH RETURN

[6] Then Naomi heard in Moab that the Lord had blessed his people in Judah by giving them good crops again. So Naomi and her daughters-in-law got ready to leave Moab to return to her homeland. [7] With her two daughters-in-law she set out from the place where she had been living, and they took the road that would lead them back to Judah.

[8] But on the way, Naomi said to her two daughters-in-law, "Go back to your mothers' homes. And may the Lord reward you for your kindness to your husbands and to me. [9] May the Lord bless you with the security of another marriage." Then she kissed them good-bye, and they all broke down and wept.

[10] "No," they said. "We want to go with you to your people." [11] But Naomi replied, "Why should you go on with me? Can I still give birth to other sons who could grow up to be your husbands? [12] No, my daughters, return to your parents' homes, for I am too old to marry again. And even if it were possible, and I were to get married tonight and bear sons, then what? [13] Would you wait for them to grow up and refuse to marry someone else? No, of course not, my daughters! Things are far more bitter for me than for you, because the Lord himself has raised his fist against me." [14] And again they wept together, and Orpah kissed her mother-in-law good-bye.

But Ruth clung tightly to Naomi. [15] "Look," Naomi said to her, "your sister-in-law has gone back to her people and to her gods. You should do the same." [16] But Ruth replied, "Don't ask me to leave you and turn back. Wherever you go, I will go; wherever you live, I will live. Your people will be my people, and your God will be my God. [17] Wherever you die, I will die, and there I will be buried. May the Lord punish me severely if I allow anything but death to separate us!" [18] When Naomi saw that Ruth was determined to go with her, she said nothing more.

[19] So the two of them continued on their journey. When they came to Bethlehem, the entire town was excited by their arrival. "Is it really Naomi?" the women asked. [20] "Don't call me Naomi," she responded. "Instead, call me Mara, for the Almighty has made life very bitter for me. [21] I went away full, but the Lord has brought me home empty. Why call me Naomi when the Lord has caused me to suffer and the Almighty has sent such tragedy upon me?"

[22] So Naomi returned from Moab, accompanied by
her daughter-in-law Ruth, the young Moabite woman.
They arrived in Bethlehem in late spring, at the
beginning of the barley harvest.

2

RUTH WORKS IN BOAZ'S FIELD

[1] Now there was a wealthy and influential man in Bethlehem named Boaz, who was a relative of Naomi's husband, Elimelech. [2] One day Ruth the Moabite said to Naomi, "Let me go out into the harvest fields to pick up the stalks of grain left behind by anyone who is kind enough to let me do it." Naomi replied, "All right, my daughter, go ahead."

[3] So Ruth went out to gather grain behind the harvesters. And as it happened, she found herself working in a field that belonged to Boaz, the relative of her father-in-law, Elimelech. [4] While she was there, Boaz arrived from Bethlehem and greeted the harvesters. "The Lord be with you!" he said. "The Lord bless you!" the harvesters replied.

[5] Then Boaz asked his foreman, "Who is that young woman over there? Who does she belong to?" [6] And the foreman replied, "She is the young woman from Moab who came back with Naomi. [7] She asked me this morning if she could gather grain behind the harvesters. She has been hard at work ever since, except for a few minutes' rest in the shelter."

[8] Boaz went over and said to Ruth, "Listen, my daughter. Stay right here with us when you gather grain; don't go to any other fields. Stay right behind the young women working in my field. [9] See which part of the field they are harvesting, and then follow them. I have warned the young men not to treat you roughly. And when you are thirsty, help yourself to the water they have drawn from the well." [10] Ruth fell at his feet and thanked him warmly. "What have I done to deserve such kindness?" she asked. "I am only a foreigner." [11] "Yes, I know," Boaz replied. "But I also know about everything you have done for your mother-in-law since the death of your husband. I have heard how you left your father and mother and your own land to live here among complete strangers. [12] May the Lord, the God of Israel, under whose wings you have come to take refuge, reward you fully for what you have done."

[13] "I hope I continue to lease you, sir," she replied. "You have comforted me by speaking so kindly to me, even though I am not one of your workers."

[14] At mealtime Boaz called to her, "Come over here, and help yourself to some food. You can dip your bread in the sour wine." So she sat with his harvesters, and Boaz gave her some roasted grain to eat. She ate all she wanted and still had some left over.

[15] When Ruth went back to work again, Boaz ordered his young men, "Let her gather grain right among the sheaves without stopping her. [16] And pull out some heads of barley from the bundles and drop them on purpose for her. Let her pick them up, and don't give her a hard time!"

[17] So Ruth gathered barley there all day, and when she beat out the grain that evening, it filled an entire basket. [18] She carried it back into town and showed it to her mother-in-law. Ruth also gave her the roasted grain that was left over from her meal. [19] "Where did you gather all this grain today?" Naomi asked. "Where did you work? May the Lord bless the one who helped you!"

So Ruth told her mother-in-law about the man in whose field she had worked. She said, "The man I worked with today is named Boaz." [20] "May the Lord bless him!" Naomi told her daughter-in-law. "He is showing his kindness to us as well as to your dead husband. That man is one of our closest relatives, one of our family redeemers."

[21] Then Ruth said, "What's more, Boaz even told me to come back and stay with his harvesters until the entire harvest is completed." [22] "Good!" Naomi exclaimed. "Do as he said, my daughter. Stay with his young women right through the whole harvest. You might be harassed in other fields, but you'll be safe with him." [23] So Ruth worked alongside the women in Boaz's fields and gathered grain with them until the end of the barley harvest. Then she continued working with them through the wheat harvest in early summer. And all the while she lived with her mother-in-law.

3

RUTH AT THE THRESHING FLOOR

[1] One day Naomi said to Ruth, "My daughter, it's time that I found a permanent home for you, so that you will be provided for. [2] Boaz is a close relative of ours, and he's been very kind by letting you gather grain with his young women. Tonight he will be winnowing barley at the threshing floor. [3] Now do as I tell you—take a bath and put on perfume and dress in your nicest clothes. Then go to the threshing floor, but don't let Boaz see you until he has finished eating and drinking. [4] Be sure to notice where he lies down; then go and uncover his feet and lie down there. He will tell you what to do." [5] "I will do everything you say," Ruth replied.

[6] So she went down to the threshing floor that night and followed the instructions of her mother-in-law.

[7] After Boaz had finished eating and drinking and was in good spirits, he lay down at the far end of the pile of grain and went to sleep. Then Ruth came quietly, uncovered his feet, and lay down. [8] Around midnight Boaz suddenly woke up and turned over. He was surprised to find a woman lying at his feet! [9] "Who are you?" he asked. "I am your servant Ruth," she replied. "Spread the corner of your covering over me, for you are my family redeemer."

[10] "The Lord bless you, my daughter!" Boaz exclaimed. "You are showing even more family loyalty now than you did before, for you have not gone after a younger man, whether rich or poor. [11] Now don't worry about a thing, my daughter. I will do what is necessary, for everyone in town knows you are a virtuous woman.

¹² But while it's true that I am one of your family redeemers, there is another man who is more closely related to you than I am. ¹³ Stay here tonight, and in the morning I will talk to him. If he is willing to redeem you, very well. Let him marry you. But if he is not willing, then as surely as the Lord lives, I will redeem you myself! Now lie down here until morning."

[14] So Ruth lay at Boaz's feet until the morning, but she got up before it was light enough for people to recognize each other. For Boaz had said, "No one must know that a woman was here at the threshing floor." [15] Then Boaz said to her, "Bring your cloak and spread it out." He measured six scoops of barley into the cloak and placed it on her back. Then he returned to the town.

[16] When Ruth went back to her mother-in-law, Naomi asked, "What happened, my daughter?"

Ruth told Naomi everything Boaz had done for her, [17] and she added, "He gave me these six scoops of barley and said, 'Don't go back to your mother-in-law empty-handed.'"

[18] Then Naomi said to her, "Just be patient, my daughter, until we hear what happens. The man won't rest until he has settled things today."

4

BOAZ MARRIES RUTH

[1] Boaz went to the town gate and took a seat there. Just then the family redeemer he had mentioned came by, so Boaz called out to him, "Come over here and sit down, friend. I want to talk to you." So they sat down together. [2] Then Boaz called ten leaders from the town and asked them to sit as witnesses.

[3] And Boaz said to the family redeemer, "You know Naomi, who came back from Moab. She is selling the land that belonged to our relative Elimelech. [4] I thought I should speak to you about it so that you can redeem it if you wish. If you want the land, then buy it here in the presence of these witnesses. But if you don't want it, let me know right away, because I am next in line to redeem it after you."

The man replied, "All right, I'll redeem it." [5] Then Boaz told him, "Of course, your purchase of the land from Naomi also requires that you marry Ruth, the Moabite widow. That way she can have children who will carry on her husband's name and keep the land in the family."

[6] "Then I can't redeem it," the family redeemer replied, "because this might endanger my own estate. You redeem the land; I cannot do it."

[7] Now in those days it was the custom in Israel for anyone transferring a right of purchase to remove his sandal and hand it to the other party. This publicly validated the transaction. [8] So the other family redeemer drew off his sandal as he said to Boaz, "You buy the land."

[9] Then Boaz said to the elders and to the crowd standing around, "You are witnesses that today I have bought from Naomi all the property of Elimelech, Kilion, and Mahlon. [10] And with the land I have acquired Ruth, the Moabite widow of Mahlon, to be my wife. This way she can have a son to carry on the family name of her dead husband and to inherit the family property here in his hometown. You are all witnesses today."

¹¹ Then the elders and all the people standing in the gate replied, "We are witnesses! May the Lord make this woman who is coming into your home like Rachel and Leah, from whom all the nation of Israel descended! May you prosper in Ephrathah and be famous in Bethlehem. ¹² And may the Lord give you descendants by this young woman who will be like those of our ancestor Perez, the son of Tamar and Judah."

THE DESCENDANTS OF BOAZ

[13] So Boaz took Ruth into his home, and she became his wife. When he slept with her, the Lord enabled her to become pregnant, and she gave birth to a son. [14] Then the women of the town said to Naomi, "Praise the Lord, who has now provided a redeemer for your family! May this child be famous in Israel. [15] May he restore your youth and care for you in your old age. For he is the son of your daughter-in-law who loves you and has been better to you than seven sons!"

¹⁶ Naomi took the baby and cuddled him to her breast. And she cared for him as if he were her own. ¹⁷ The neighbor women said, "Now at last Naomi has a son again!" And they named him Obed. He became the father of Jesse and the grandfather of David.

[18] This is the genealogical record of their ancestor Perez:

Perez was the father of Hezron.
[19] Hezron was the father of Ram.
Ram was the father of Amminadab.
[20] Amminadab was the father of Nahshon.
Nahshon was the father of Salmon.
[21] Salmon was the father of Boaz.
Boaz was the father of Obed.
[22] Obed was the father of Jesse.
Jesse was the father of David.

ALABASTER

TYLER ZAK
Product Manager, Art Director

MATTHEW RAVENELLE
Layout Designer

SAMUEL HAN
Studio Manager, Editor

DANIEL HAN
Studio Stylist

ALEXIS SOOMIN LEE
Studio Assistant

ZACH MCKINLEY
Cover Image

BRYAN YE-CHUNG
Co-Founder, Creative Director

BRIAN CHUNG
Co-Founder, Managing Director

WILLA JIN
Operations Director

EMALY HUNTER
Customer Experience Specialist

DARIN MCKENNA
Content Editor

JOSEPHINE LAW
Original Designer

 ALABASTER

PHOTOGRAPHERS

Andriana Kovalchuk
Brian Wu
Chester Nathanael Wright
Echo Yun Chen
Ellie Lee
Emily DiBrito
Eric Natividad
Haven Kim
Ian Teraoka
Janna Christian
JaWan Johnson

Joel Rojas
Jonathan Knepper
Lois Lee
Makito Umekita
Marleth Tatad
Mike Sunu
Naomi Zaki
Salomé Watel
Samuel Han
Sophia Hsin
Zach Mckinley

MODELS

Alexis Soomin Lee
Ashanti Plummer
Daniel Han
Esther Kim
So Seol Shin

CONTINUE THE CONVERSATION

www.alabasterco.com